Sue Coombes

Define — LC
explain
apply
conclude.

LAW CARTOONS

AUSTRALIA
The Law Book Company
Brisbane • Sydney • Melbourne • Perth

CANADA
Carswell
Ottawa • Toronto • Calgary • Montreal • Vancouver

AGENTS
Steimatzky's Agency Ltd., Tel Aviv;
N.M. Tripathi (Private) Ltd., Bombay;
Eastern Law House (Private) Ltd., Calcutta;
M.P.P. House, Bangalore;
Universal Book Traders, Delhi;
Aditya Books, Delhi;
MacMillan Shuppan KK, Tokyo;
Pakistan Law House, Karachi, Lahore

LAW CARTOONS

by

Susan Tayfoor, LL.B.

Lecturer, Birkbeck College

First Edition

LONDON
SWEET & MAXWELL
1995

Published in 1995 by
Sweet & Maxwell Limited
100 Avenue Road, Swiss Cottage
London NW3 3PF
http://www.smlawpub.co.uk
Printed in Great Britain by the Headway Press Ltd.
Reprinted 1998

A CIP catalogue record for this book
is available from the British Library.

ISBN 0421 538104

All rights reserved. UK statutory material in this publication is acknowledged as Crown copyright. No part of this publication may be reproduced or transmitted in any form or by any means, or stored in any retrieval system of any nature without prior written permission, except for permitted fair dealing under the Copyright, Designs and Patents Act 1988, or in accordance with the terms of a licence issued by the Copyright Licensing Agency in respect of photocopying and/or reprographic reproduction. Application for permission for other use of copyright material including permission to reproduce extracts in other published works shall be made to the publishers. Full acknowledgement of author, publisher and source must be given.

No natural forests were destroyed to make this product only farmed timber was used and re-planted.

© Sweet & Maxwell 1995

This book is dedicated to my grandparents, Eileen and Jack, with much love and thanks for their support and encouragement.

Susan Tayfoor 1995

Preface

Law is a subject which for many people still conjures up Dickensian images of cramped, ill-lit chambers, and bewigged lawyers sitting behind piles of dusty textbooks.

I wanted to sweep those images away, and make law much more accessible to readers, by presenting each subject in an enjoyable way.

In writing this series, I wanted to show the reader that studying law can be both entertaining and informative. In doing so, I did not wish to over simplify the subject for the student. By presenting the material in a visual way, it can be understood and remembered much more easily than in traditional textbook form.

This series aims to cover the basic principles of law, without becoming caught up in too much detail. I hope this series will open up law as a subject to many more readers, and above all, lighten the student's workload!

London, April 1995

A Foreword...

The Characters in Tort Law

The Plaintiff

Is the wronged party bringing the action

The Defendant

Is the party who may or may not be liable

The Judge

Has the power to grant damages, an injunction, or specific performance where appropriate.

Warning! This book is not intended as a legal bible. If you are thinking of conducting your own court case, you would be advised to supplement your reading with a sturdy textbook.

CONTENTS

Glossary : Some Legal Terms

Chapter One : TRESPASS TO THE PERSON

Chapter Two : NEGLIGENCE - The Duty of Care

Chapter Three : NEGLIGENCE - Breach of Duty

Chapter Four : NEGLIGENCE - That Results in Damage

Chapter Five : THE DEFENCES

Chapter Six : THE OCCUPIER'S LIABILITY ACTS

Chapter Seven : NUISANCE

Chapter Eight : TRESPASS TO LAND AND TO GOODS

Chapter Nine : STRICT LIABILITY

Chapter Ten : VICARIOUS LIABILITY

Chapter Eleven : THE EMPLOYER'S DUTY

Chapter Twelve : DEFAMATION

GLOSSARY OF SOME LEGAL TERMS

> A TORT ... is a civil wrong, which gives the plaintiff the right to bring an action in the civil courts (eg. for nuisance, trespass etc.)

CONTRIBUTORY NEGLIGENCE ... If someone is contributorily negligent, this means that in some way, they made the damages they suffered worse.

NOVUS ACTUS INTERVENIENS ... Is when a new act intervenes, and breaks the chain of causation so the original person is no longer liable for the end result.

RES IPSA LOQUITUR ... Is a rule of evidence meaning the plaintiff will ask the court to make a finding of negligence, and leave it up to the defendant to disprove it.

THE STANDARD OF PROOF ... Is how much proof is needed to establish a fact. In civil cases, the standard of proof is the _balance of probabilities_. The person wishing to prove a fact must show that it is more likely than not that it happened this way.

STRICT LIABILITY ... Someone may be liable for a tort, even though they took all possible care to avoid it. This type of liability is called strict liability, and is usually imposed to protect the general public from harmful acts.

VICARIOUS LIABILITY ... To be vicariously liable for the torts of another, means to be responsible for the torts of another, because of a special relationship - for example, an employer may be vicariously liable for the torts of an employee, and the plaintiff could sue either of them.

VOLENTI NON FIT INJURIA ... This is a claim, by way of defence, that the plaintiff was aware of the risk, and was willing to take it, therefore the defendant is not responsible for the consequences.

And finally, some remedies you may be granted...

damages - In the form of money, given to compensate you for your loss

specific performance - Is a court order to the defendant, to do something.

injunction - Is a court order to the defendant, to stop doing something.

CHAPTER ONE - TRESPASS TO THE PERSON - Assault

Contrary to common belief, to assault someone is to cause them to fear physical violence. Once you touch them, it's battery.

one legal definition of assault is...

> an act of the defendant which causes the plaintiff reasonable apprehension of the infliction of a battery on him by the defendant.
> — Winfield & Jolowicz, p.54

There are many ways you can assault someone without touching them...

By threatening words...

By shaking your fist in a threatening manner...

By pointing a gun at them...

It is also possible to assault someone with a harmless object, since the essential element in assault is fear...

On 20th January 1991, a man was jailed for six years, for attempting to rob a bank ... with a banana.

The robbery was committed on the day he finished a prison sentence for the same offence.

The Times January 21 1991

Battery

Is the direct and intentional application of physical force to another
(without lawful justification)

Any physical contact may equal "force"

a possible battery may be...
- to spit at someone
- to pour water over them
- to snatch a chair away as they sit down
- to take a person's fingerprints without observing the statutory requirements (Magistrates Courts Act 1952, s. 40)

However, a certain amount of contact in everyday life would not amount to battery

e.g. "Don't push!" — jostling in a queue

 "Ow!" — or stepping on someone's foot in a crowded place

In the words of Lord Devlin... "The jostler, the back-slapper and the hand-shaker" would not be liable for battery

---

So does the defendant have to intend to harm the plaintiff?

According to Lord Goff, the act does not have to be hostile, so...

F v. West Berkshire Health Authority 1989

"A prank which misfires, or an over-friendly slap on the back" are all prima facie actionable

False Imprisonment

Someone can be falsely imprisoned...  in a car in the street  on a roof

...In fact, anywhere where they are wrongfully deprived of their liberty to go where they please.

 When are they not wrongfully deprived of their liberty?

- When the restraint is reasonable, ie the plaintiff refuses to pay an exit fee.
- When the defendant merely refuses to help the plaintiff leave the premises
- When a manager holds a suspected shoplifter for a reasonable length of time to investigate.

The person imprisoned can even be unaware of it at the time

"I think a person can be imprisoned whilst asleep, whilst in a state of drunkenness, and whilst he is a lunatic"  Atkin LJ

But the restraint has to be total. If there is a reasonable means of escape available, the plaintiff can't claim to be falsely imprisoned.

NB. Assault
      Battery   } All make up the tort of Trespass to the Person
      False Imprisonment

Each one is actionable *per se*  so there's no need to prove damage

Defences

"Are there any defences to trespass to the person?"

"Yes 1) Consent 2) Lawful arrest 3) Self defence"

Except Where the blow in self defence is out of all proportion to the attack

And a citizen's lawful arrest will not be lawful if the offence has not yet been committed.

"But he stamped on my foot!"

"So when can I make a lawful arrest?"

Police and Criminal Evidence Act 1984

A person may, without warrant arrest any person who is or who he suspects with reasonable cause to be, in the act of committing an arrestable offence s. 24 (4)

or when the arrestable offence has been committed s. 24 (5)

Exception

At common law, a person may take reasonable steps to stop or prevent an actual or reasonably apprehended breach of the peace.

Albert v. Lavin 1982

QUIZ - TRESPASS TO THE PERSON

① If someone points a gun at you, which you knew was unloaded, you could nonetheless sue them for assault.

   True / False ?

② Someone tells you your spouse has had a terrible accident. It's a malicious lie, and leaves you suffering from nervous shock. However, there is nothing you can do about it.

   True / False ?

③ If someone plants an uninvited kiss on your cheek, you can sue them for battery.

   True / False ?

④ Someone is about to attack you, and you knock him unconscious. You cannot claim the blow was in self-defence as you hit him first.

   True / False ?

⑤ Your employer dismisses you, then refuses to let you into the work-place to collect your belongings. You could consider bringing an action for false imprisonment.

   True / False ?

CHAPTER TWO: NEGLIGENCE - The Duty of Care

"What *is* negligence?"

Negligence can be — a way of committing an act
— or a separate, independent tort

Negligence was established as a separate, independent tort in 1932...

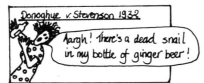

Donoghue v. Stevenson 1932

"Aargh! There's a dead snail in my bottle of ginger beer!"

Mrs Donoghue suffered illness as a result of this, and took the manufacturers to court...

It was held that they were liable in tort, and they owed a duty to her, as the ultimate consumer, to take care she was not injured by a negligently manufactured product.

In the above case, Lord Atkin laid down the famous "Neighbour Principle"

"You must take reasonable care to avoid acts or omissions which you can reasonably foresee would be likely to injure your neighbour. Who then in law, is my neighbour? ... persons who are so closely and directly affected by my act that I ought reasonably to have them in my contemplation as being so affected."

Not every careless act will count as negligence...

> It is not for every careless act that a man may be held responsible in law, nor even for every careless act that causes damage. He will only be liable in negligence if he is under a legal duty to take care
>
> — Winfield & Jolowicz

There are three elements which must be proved, to show someone is liable in negligence...
- They owed a duty of care
- That duty was breached
- That as a result of this breach, the plaintiff suffered damage

The courts will consider all these factors, before deciding that a duty of care was owed
- Was the harm reasonably foreseeable?
- What was the proximity of relationship between the parties?
- Would it be just and reasonable to impose a duty?
- public policy

However, the type of damage caused by the negligent act is not always recoverable, especially in the cases of...
a) Pure Economic Loss
b) Negligent Misstatement
c) Nervous Shock

Pure Economic Loss

 "What is pure economic loss?"

Spartan Steel & Alloys Ltd v. Martin & Co (Contractors) Ltd 1973

 "Whoops! We've just cut off the factory's power supply..."

 factory owners: "Because of that, metal being melted in a furnace is ruined. We're also wasting time when we could be doing more melts."

The plaintiffs claimed...

£368 for damage to metal in the furnace
£400 for loss of profit on sale of that metal
£1,767 for loss of profit for four future melts.

Held: The £1,767 was financial loss, not directly connected to any physical damage. It was therefore not recoverable, being PURE ECONOMIC LOSS.

"Why is pure economic loss not recoverable?"

Because to allow such claims may result in

 Cardozo CJ: "Liability in an indeterminate amount for an indeterminate time to an indeterminate class."

Ultramares Corporation v. Touche 1931

To claim for economic loss, it must be linked to physical damage, except in the case of Negligent Misstatement...

Negligent Misstatement

If you suffer financial loss, after being badly advised, can the person who advised you be liable in negligence?

You may be able to recover the loss, so long as...
1) A special relationship exists (eg. solicitor and client)
2) The plaintiff relies on the defendant's skill and knowledge
3) It was reasonable for him to rely on the advice

Hedley Byrne & Co v. Heller & Partners 1964

This test was qualified in...

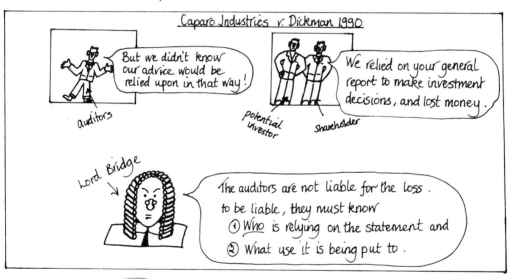

In one recent case, a woman was allowed to recover the money she'd lost on a secondhand car, from a friend, who'd wrongly advised her to buy it.

Chaudhry v. Prabhaker 1988

Nervous Shock

A careless driver runs over her son. Can she sue the driver if she suffers nervous shock as a result?

First of all, what *is* nervous shock?

It's more than just grief or depression.
Lord Ackner defined it as...

"The sudden appreciation by sight or sound of a horrifying event"

This must result in a psychiatric or physical illness to be recoverable.

To claim for nervous shock, you must fall into one of these two categories
- an unwilling participant in the event
- or a passive, unwilling witness

Not all witnesses to a shocking event can claim for nervous shock as shown in <u>Alcock v. Chief Constable of South Yorkshire 1991</u>

"We're all friends or relatives of people killed in the fire in Bradford football stadium"

Who could claim for nervous shock?

"Only those who were close relatives AND who were temporally and spatially close to the accident, or its immediate aftermath."

QUIZ - NEGLIGENCE - The Duty of Care

① A woman's family were involved in a terrible road accident. When she was told about it an hour later, she rushed to the hospital and suffered nervous shock as a result of seeing them in a terrible state. Could she bring an action against the negligent driver.   Yes / No ?

② Someone sees their estranged brother involved in an accident. They hadn't spoken for over ten years, but the brother could claim for nervous shock nonetheless.   True / False ?

③ Liability may arise if someone watched their property burn down as a result of negligence, and suffered nervous shock as a result.   True / False ?

④ A barrister can be sued for negligence if she/he conducts a case badly in court.   True / False ?

⑤ If you see someone drowning, and don't try to rescue them, you may be liable in negligence.   True / False ?

CHAPTER THREE: NEGLIGENCE - Breach of Duty

When will our actions be considered negligent?

> Negligence is the omission to do something which a reasonable man... would do, or doing something which a prudent and reasonable man would not do. — Alderson B

Blyth v. Birmingham Waterworks Co. 1856

All our actions are compared to those of an ordinary reasonable man, who is neither careless, nor overly careful.

What is appropriate will depend on the circumstances, and what a reasonable man would have done. However...

Lord Macmillan: "What to one judge may seem far fetched may seem to another both natural and probable"

Glasgow Corporation v. Muir 1943

The duty of care is breached when we fall below the standard expected of an ordinary reasonable man.

The test is objective, which means surprising results are sometimes reached...

"A learner driver should be judged by the standard of an ordinary, experienced driver."

Nettleship v. Weston 1971

What sort of precautions against the risk would an ordinary, reasonable man take?

Behaviour regarding the risk is weighed against...

- The magnitude of the risk
- The social utility of the action
- The cost of taking precautionary measures

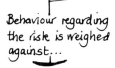

You can't be expected to take precautions against every single risk, especially if the risk is minimal, but...

The more serious the risk, the more precautions are necessary > and vice versa

The duty of care is owed to each person individually

> In assessing the magnitude of the risk it is important to notice that (if) the plaintiff suffers from some disability which increases the magnitude of the risk to him, that disability must be taken into account
> — Winfield & Jolowicz [134]

for example, in *Paris v. Stepney Borough Council 1951*

I was blind in one eye, and now I'm blind in both, because my employers failed to supply me with protective goggles.

But we don't supply any of our workers with goggles.

Well, you should have taken his disability into account, and taken more precautions in his case.

The social utility of the activity is also something which must be taken into account. In the words of Asquith LJ...

As has often been pointed out, if all the trains in this country were restricted to a speed of five miles an hour, there would be fewer accidents, but our national life would be intolerably slowed down.

Daborn Bath Tramways 1946

Sometimes it will be considered reasonable to take an abnormal risk

The purpose to be served, if sufficiently important, justifies the assumption of an abnormal risk

for example...

Watt v. Hertfordshire County Council 1954

Fireman: I was injured in a lorry, by a heavy jack, while travelling to an emergency

We had to drive out in a hurry, to rescue a woman trapped under a bus. There was no time to secure the jack properly.

Denning LJ: Saving life and limb justifies a considerable risk being taken.

Different Standards of Care

CHILDREN

Are children responsible for their torts?

Yes, but they will be judged by the standard expected of a reasonable child of that age.

Skilled Workers / Professionals

A doctor must show the skill of a reasonably competent doctor, a surgeon should show the skill of a reasonably competent surgeon, etc.

The "Bolam" test for professional negligence:

A professional person...

...is not guilty of negligence if he has acted in accordance with a practice accepted as proper by a reasonable body of medical men skilled in that particular art.

Bolam v. Friern Hospital 1957

The DIY Enthusiast

If a person makes repairs around the house, they will be expected to show the skill of a person reasonably competent in that area, but not of a professional workman.

If however, the work is particularly complicated, and may be dangerous if not done properly, that person will be expected to show the skill of a professional, or to hire an expert.

QUIZ - NEGLIGENCE - Breach of Duty

① A man who unknowingly suffered a minor stroke whilst driving, could not be liable for negligence if he was then involved in an accident.

True / False ?

② Heavy rain made a factory floor slippery with oil and water. Try as they might, the owners couldn't keep it completely dry, and someone slipped and was injured. Were the factory owners negligent?

Yes / No ?

③ A junior doctor makes a mistake which an experienced doctor would not make. However, the standard they are judged by will take their junior status into account.

Yes / No ?

④ A woman walking past a cricket ground was struck on the head by a cricket ball. It was foreseeable, but unlikely that this might happen, and a seven foot fence had been put up round the cricket ground, but there was still a slight risk. Were the defendants negligent?

Yes / No ?

CHAPTER FOUR : NEGLIGENCE - That Results in Damage

The 'but for' test is used to decide whether the breach of duty was the cause (or a material cause) of the damage.

As Lord Denning put it...

"If the damage would not have happened but for a particular fault, then that fault is the cause of the damage. If it would have happened just the same, fault or no fault, the fault is not the cause of the damage"

Cork v. Kirby MacLean Ltd 1952

The plaintiff must show the damage was caused by the defendant's negligence...

"I'm blind because the hospital was negligent"

Excess oxygen given negligently at birth was a possible cause of the plaintiff's damaged sight

The plaintiff's claim failed because she couldn't prove the hospital's negligence was the main cause of her damaged sight.

Wilsher v. Essex Area Health Authority 1988

If the outcome would have been the same, negligent act or no negligent act, the defendant will not be liable...

 "I feel ill, please examine me"   "No. Go home and see your doctor tomorrow"

The patient went home and died of arsenic poisoning.

Held: The casualty officer's refusal to examine him was not the cause of his death. Even if he had examined him, it would have been too late to save him.

Barnett v. Chelsea and West Kensington Hospital Management Committee

The 'but for' test is not always appropriate, however.

 for example: A and B both fatally shoot C at the same time. By applying the 'But for' test, neither of them would be the cause of C's death.

When there is a problem of multiple causation, the courts have taken a different view:

The plaintiff's leg was injured by a negligent driver, in a road accident.

Then later, there was a robbery, the plaintiff was shot in the same injured leg, which had to be amputated.

Held: The negligent driver must pay damages for the injured leg, even after it was later amputated.

Baker v. Willoughby 1970

However, in a later case it was held that if the second event had occurred naturally (and had been unconnected with the first event) it may be unfair to expect defendants to pay beyond the second injury.

Jobling v. Associated Dairies 1982

The plaintiff suffered injury to his back, because of an accident at work. The employers were ordered to pay compensation.

Three years later, the plaintiff developed myelopathy (a totally unconnected illness, also affecting the back). The employers no longer had to pay compensation for the initial injury.

 "This would put the plaintiff in a better position than he would have been."

Novus Actus Interveniens

A novus actus interveniens is a new, intervening act, which breaks the chain of causation. In this case, the defendant may claim that he is no longer liable for the events that follow.

The intervening act may be by the plaintiff

The plaintiff's leg would give way unexpectedly, as a result of an injury at work. One day...

"Leave me alone, I'll manage by myself!"

He fell, fracturing his ankle, and claimed that the fall was a result of the initial injury.

"You were unreasonable in refusing help to go down the stairs. That refusal constituted a novus actus interveniens"

McKew v. Holland & Hannen & Cubitts (Scotland) Ltd 1969

Or it may be by a third party.

In any case, as Lord Wright observed

"To break the chain of causation it must be shown that there is... a new cause which disturbs the sequence of events, something which can be described as either unreasonable or extraneous or extrinsic."

The Oropesa 1943

 "When will an intervening act _not_ break the chain of causation?"

 "When it was done instinctively, in response to an emergency, or where it was reasonably foreseeable, and should have been guarded against."

Res Ipsa Loquitur

Who must prove negligence?

The Standard of Proof

Usually the plaintiff must prove it was <u>more likely than not</u> that the accident was caused by the defendant's negligence.

But I don't know how the accident happened, how can I prove it was due to the defendant's negligence?

You may be able to rely on the maxim "Res Ipsa Loquitur" meaning "the thing speaks for itself."

Res Ipsa Loquitur is a rule of evidence which means that from the facts, the court may assume the defendant was negligent, and leave it up to the defendant to rebut (disprove) this.

For example, in <u>Scott v. London and St Katherine Docks 1865</u>

I was hit on the head by six falling bags of sugar. I can't prove how it happened, or if the defendant was negligent but sugar bags don't normally fall from the sky, so I'm relying on the maxim Res Ipsa Loquitur.

To rely on this maxim the following conditions must be met:

① There must be no explanation from the defendant as to how the accident happened.

② The thing causing the damage must have been under the defendant's control.

③ The accident must have been something which wouldn't normally happen without negligence.

Remoteness of Damage

Even if the defendant's negligent act caused the damage, if it was too remote he may not be liable.

> No defendant is responsible ad infinitum for all the consequences of his wrongful conducts... the law must draw a line somewhere.
> — Winfield & Jolowicz

There are two differing views on how far you will be held responsible for your actions

The Test of Directness
You are responsible for whatever happens as a direct consequence of your actions, even if the result was unforeseeable.
— Re Polemis 1921

The Test of Reasonable Foresight
You are responsible for what happens, providing the damage was a type which could have been foreseen.
— The Wagon Mound 1961

The later view is now favoured by the courts. As Viscount Simonds stated in the later case...

> It does not seem consonant with current ideas of justice or morality that for an act of negligence, however slight or venial, which results in some trivial foreseeable damage the actor should be liable for all consequences however unforeseeable and however grave, so long as they can be said to be direct

To be liable then, the damage must have been foreseeable. Once it was foreseeable, however, it makes no difference if it was greater than expected.

This rule is subject to an exception...

The 'Egg Shell Skull' Rule

 If I cause foreseeable injury to a person, I may be liable for all the consequences of that injury, whether they were foreseeable or not.

---

for example...

 My husband committed suicide, due to a depression brought on by an injury at work.

 employers → Well that's hardly our fault!

 Yes it is. Your negligence caused his injury at work, and set off a chain of events, resulting in his suicide. You are liable for this under the 'egg shell skull' principle.

<u>Pigney v. Pointer's Transport Services Ltd 1957</u>

In a case in 1986, a drunken driver had an accident, injuring his passenger. The passenger suffered brain damage, and a permanent personality change as a result.

 By the time the action came to court, the plaintiff had committed sexual offences and rape, as a result of the personality change, and was sentenced to life imprisonment.

 Am I liable for all these events, or is the personality change and prison sentence too remote?

The plaintiff was liable for all these events, under the 'egg shell skull' principle.

<u>Meah v. McCreamer 1986</u>

QUIZ - NEGLIGENCE - That Results in Damage

① A manhole was left uncovered in the street, with paraffin lamps around it. A small boy, playing nearby, knocked one of the lamps into the manhole, which exploded, badly burning him. The explosion was not foreseeable, although injury by burning was. Would the defendants be liable?
     Yes / No

② A throws a lit firework at B, who panics and throws it at C where it explodes, injuring him. A will be able to claim that B's act was a 'novus actus interveniens'.   True / False?

③ If someone is injured by A, and then receives negligent medical treatment, resulting in worse injury, A will be able to claim the negligent treatment amounted to a 'novus actus interveniens'.
     True / False?

④ B is decorating a house for the owner who is away. While B goes to the shops, he leaves the house unlocked and comes back to find someone broke in and stole a diamond bracelet. Will B be liable for the theft?   Yes / No.

CHAPTER FIVE: THE DEFENCES - Contributory Negligence

defendant: "He was partly to blame!"

The defendant's liability for damages will be reduced if he can show that the plaintiff...

Lord Simon: "did not in his own interest take reasonable care of himself, and contributed by this want of care, to his own injury."

Nance v. British Colombia Electric Ry PC 1951

How much should the plaintiff's damages be reduced?

section 1(1), Law Reform (Contributory Negligence) Act 1945

"To such an extent as the court thinks just and equitable having regard to the claimant's share in the responsibility for the damage."

The usual maximum reduction is 25 per cent when injuries could have been avoided altogether if the plaintiff had taken due care.

Some examples of Contributory Negligence

- Stepping in front of a fast moving car
- Riding without a seat-belt
- Taking a lift with a drunk driver

The Woman who was Trapped in a Toilet.
She tried to climb out but fell off a toilet roll holder. She was held to be contributorily negligent in her manner of trying to escape.

Sayers v. Harlow UDC 1958

Volenti Non Fit Injuria

By agreeing to the risk, or to running the risk of harm, you cannot afterwards sue for any damage you suffered as a result of agreeing to it.

for example...

If someone rugby-tackled you in the street, you could sue for assault and battery, but not however, if you were both in a game of rugby.

or if someone cut open your stomach this defence would apply if you'd consented to an operation.

If the risk exceeded the risk you'd consented to, it would be actionable.

Smith v. Baker 1891

Mere knowledge of the risk did not mean the plaintiff had consented to the risk

As Lord Denning said...

"There must be... evidence that the plaintiff has expressly or impliedly agreed to waive his right of action"

Nettleship v. Weston 1971

In the above case, the plaintiff gave driving lessons to a learner driver, who crashed the car. Getting into the car did not amount to volenti non fit injuria, or consenting to the risk.

Volenti Non fit Injuria and RESCUERS

If someone is injured while they were rushing to the rescue, can they be said to have consented to the risk?

A policeman was injured by a horse falling on him while he was rushing to stop it bolting into a busy street

Since he'd acted in response to an emergency which arose since the defendant had left the horses unattended, the policeman couldn't be said to have voluntarily assumed the risk

Haynes v. Harwood 1935

If, however, the horse had bolted across an empty field, where there was no risk of harm to anyone, the defence of volenti non fit injuria would apply

What's the difference between a plea of contributory negligence, and of volenti non fit injuria?

Contributory negligence means the courts can apportion the damage, holding the plaintiff responsible for some loss, and the defendant for the rest.
Volenti non fit injuria however, is a complete defence, meaning the defendant is not liable at all.

Ex Turpi Causa Non Oritur Actio

No action can be founded on an illegal act.

This defence to an action says that if someone was breaking the law when a wrong was done to them, they may not be allowed to claim damages...

for example

a burglar who was bitten by a guard dog

or

someone who starts a fight and gets more than he bargained for

...would not be able to claim for damages

(according to Lord Denning)

For example, in _Ashton v. Turner 1981_.

Both men were escaping from a robbery, when the driver crashed the car, injuring the plaintiff (who was the passenger). The plaintiff could not claim damages for negligence, since they were in the middle of a crime at the time.

However, sometimes the fact that the plaintiff is a wrongdoer will not automatically bar the claim. It depends on the nature of the wrong act, and how closely connected to it the tortious act is.

Lord Asquith

"If A and B are proceeding to the premises which they intend burglariously to enter, and before they enter them, B picks A's pocket and steals his watch, I cannot prevail on myself to believe that A could not sue in tort."

National Coal Board v. England 1954

QUIZ - DEFENCES

① A five year old boy ran out into a busy road, and was knocked over by a car. A child of that age, however, could not be held guilty of contributory negligence.
   True / False ?

② Outside a shop is a sign saying "No responsibility is accepted for accidents and injuries on our premises, caused through our negligence". A customer enters the shop, and falls through a rotten floorboard. However, since she'd seen the sign, she would be held volenti to the risk.
   True / False ?

③ A child can never be guilty of contributory negligence.
   True / False ?

④ If you accept a lift from a driver who you knew had been drinking heavily, you would be held to have consented to the risk, and if you were then involved in an accident your claim would be defeated by the maxim 'volenti non fit injuria'.
   True / False ?

CHAPTER SIX : THE OCCUPIER'S LIABILITY ACTS - The Occupier's Liability Act 1957

If a visitor injures himself or damages his property, while on your premises, you as the occupier may be liable

---

s. 2(1) "I, the occupier, owe a duty under this Act to make sure my premises are reasonably safe for visitors"

"premises" include gardens, fields, vehicles, and even a ladder

---

Who is a lawful visitor?
Anyone with express or implied permission to come on the property

for example...
a guest
a postman
a tradesman

A front path implies people have permission to walk up it, unless you put a sign forbidding this

"No Salesmen Canvassers or tradesmen"

s. 2(6) states that anyone entering under a right conferred by law will have implied permission to be on the premises

 fireman   bailiff   policeman

The occupier owes a duty of care only while the person is doing what he was invited, permitted, or reasonably expected to do.

As Scrutton LJ. commented "When you invite a person in your house to use the staircase, you do not invite him to slide down the bannisters"

Duty of Care owed to Children

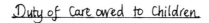

S.2(3)(a) The occupier must also be prepared for children to be less careful than adults

The corporation was held liable when the child died as a result of eating poisonous berries in the public park, because they'd put no fence or warning sign there.

Glasgow Corporation v. Taylor 1922

Duty owed to "Skilled Visitors"

If you call an electrician to your house to mend your television, you cannot be held responsible if he carelessly electrocutes himself while mending it

Lord Denning → "When a housekeeper calls in a specialist... he can reasonably expect the specialist to appreciate and guard against the dangers arising from the defect"

However, you may be liable if you were negligent in some way, or if the injury was caused in some way not connected to their work.

Ogwo v. Taylor 1988

A fireman was allowed to claim damages when he injured himself fighting a fire. This was because the occupier was careless in starting the fire.

Defences to the 1957 Act

① Excluding Liability

If they are private premises, the occupier can exclude liability if it is reasonable to do so

Please note that this defence is limited by s. 2 of the Unfair Contract Terms Act: A business can never limit its liability for death or injury caused by negligence

② Warning Notices

A warning notice will only be a defence if it was sufficient to enable the visitor to be reasonably safe   s. 2 (4)

If the visitor has no choice but to enter the danger zone, the warning sign will not be enough to escape liability.

③ Contributory Negligence

But it was partly his own fault!   Reduce his damages!

section 1 (1), Law Reform (Contributory Negligence) Act 1945

④ Volenti Non fit Injuria   s. 2(5)

He consented to the risk

ie. someone at a football match or go-karting alley, accepts any risks incidental to the game.

The Occupier's Liability Act 1984

Non-Visitor →

This Act applies to "persons other than visitors" i.e.
- trespassers
- someone exercising a private right of way
- someone in a National Park

When do I owe a duty to the non-visitor?

IF...
(a) You are aware of the danger, or have reasonable grounds to believe it exists AND
(b) You know (or suspect) the non-visitor is somewhere near the danger, or may wander into that area
(c) AND the risk is one you should reasonably protect the non-visitor against.

By the way... if the non-visitor is claiming for damage to his property, the occupier will not be liable for this, as he would be to a lawful visitor under the 1957 Act.

Do I have any Defences under the 1984 Act?

1. Putting up a clear warning sign will discharge the occupier of liability (unless the trespassers are young children)

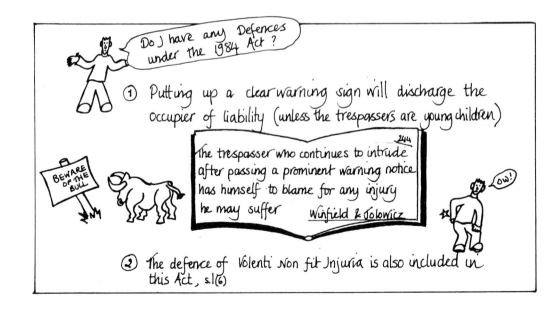

> 244
> The trespasser who continues to intrude after passing a prominent warning notice has himself to blame for any injury he may suffer — Winfield & Jolowicz

2. The defence of Volenti Non fit Injuria is also included in this Act, s.1(6)

QUIZ - OCCUPIER'S LIABILITY

① A fireman injures himself while fighting a fire on your premises. You, as the occupier, may be liable for his injuries.

                           True / False ?

② A trespasser falls over a pile of bricks left in the middle of a path, and rips his coat; can he claim for the damage to his coat under the 1984 Act?

                           Yes / No

③ Two chimney sweeps were killed by fumes from a boiler. They'd been warned about the danger, but the occupier was nonetheless liable under the 1957 Act.

                           True / False ?

④ On an occupier's land there is only one bridge to cross a river, and that bridge is in a very bad state of repair. The occupier will not be liable for injury to visitors, however, if he puts up a warning sign "This bridge is dangerous. Do not use"

                           True / False ?

CHAPTER SEVEN. NUISANCE – Public Nuisance

There are two types of nuisance, public and private. Both are torts, but public nuisance is also a crime.

Whereas private nuisance can affect only one person, public nuisance is something which materially affects a class of people.

for example...
obstructing the highway
selling unhygienic food
or
throwing fireworks in the street.

To bring an action in tort, the individual must prove especial harm

 "I suffered something over and above everyone else"

for example...
As the plaintiff drove past a golf course, a golf ball came through the windscreen, injuring his eye.
Castle v. St Augustine Links Ltd 1922

 "I could claim damages for public nuisance since I suffered especial harm"

 "I fell over an uneven paving slab, is anyone liable?"

s. 41, Highways Act 1980
Local Authorities have a duty to maintain highways, or they may be liable in public nuisance.

But note: There are several statutory defences, and as Cumming-Bruce J. once remarked

 "A highway is not to be criticised by the standards of a bowling green."

Private Nuisance

The tort of private nuisance consists of unlawful interference with the plaintiff's use or enjoyment of land

Lord Denning: The very essence of private nuisance is the unreasonable use by a man of his land, to the detriment of his neighbour

Miller v. Jackson 1972

How do I know whether my activity will count as reasonable?

It will depend on factors such as...
- time
- place
- presence/absence of malice
- whether effects are temporary or permanent

Interference with the plaintiff's enjoyment of the land may count as nuisance, if substantial, eg.

♪ through excessive noise or offensive smells

Causing physical damage to the plaintiff's property will count as nuisance, eg.

factory pollution leaving dirty smuts on washing

or

allowing sewage to collect on land

If you cannot prove physical damage to property, whether an activity is a nuisance or not, will also depend on where you live

Thesiger LJ: What would be a nuisance in Belgrave Square, would not necessarily be so in Bermondsey

Defences to Nuisance

① **Rebuttal** — "My activity is not a nuisance!"

② **Prescription** — If you've been carrying on the nuisance for over 20 years, you may have a legal right to continue doing so.

③ **Statutory Right** — "This statute permits me to carry out the activity, as long as I take reasonable care to avoid causing a nuisance"

④ **An Act of God / Act of a stranger** — as long as neither of them were foreseeable or preventable.

⑤ **Consent of the plaintiff** — "Go ahead, I don't mind"

And some not-so-valid defences...

① Claiming the plaintiff came to the nuisance is no excuse. — "I was here first!"

② "I didn't cause the nuisance, my independent contractors did, and I'm not liable for their torts" — "Nuisance is an exception, I'm afraid"

③ Adopting the nuisance — "Did you know, or should you have known of the nuisance?" "Yes" ...Then you should have taken prompt and efficient action to abate it.

QUIZ - NUISANCE

1. In private nuisance, you always need to prove damage.

    True / False

2. You buy a new house built next to a factory. The factory has been there for 25 years, and you discover it emits unpleasant fumes, and leaves dirty smuts over cars parked in the street. Since it's been there for so long, however, it's impossible to bring an action for nuisance.

    True / False

3. You store heat-sensitive paper on your premises which is easily affected by heat, and is subsequently damaged by heat coming from your neighbour's premises. Do you have a claim in nuisance?

    Yes / No

4. Blocking a pleasant view will give rise to an action for nuisance.

    True / False

CHAPTER EIGHT: TRESPASS TO LAND AND TO GOODS - Trespass to Land

Trespass to land is any unlawful entry of a person or thing onto land or buildings in the possession of another.

Salmond & Heuston define the tort of trespass as...

1) Entering upon land in the possession of the plaintiff or
2) Remaining upon such land or
3) Placing or projecting any object upon it in each case without lawful justification.

Examples of trespass are...
- leaving parcels on the wrong person's doorstep
- leaning a ladder against their wall
- throwing stones onto their land.

To trespass on land, you don't need to even step onto the land. Putting your hand through a window would be enough.

Every invasion of property, be it ever so minute, is a trespass

Entick v. Carrington 1765

You mowed my grass!

But I thought it was mine.

Basely v. Clarkson 1682

If the trespass is done voluntarily, mistake is no excuse.

Trespass can be committed without physically touching the land...

In a Tasmanian case, the defendant shot a cat, sitting on the plaintiff's roof. Shooting a bullet over the land was held to be trespass. *Davies v. Bennison 1927*

What defences are there to trespass?

① "I entered by authority of law."   eg. under PACE rights

② **Access to Neighbouring Land Act 1992**

 The court can make an order allowing access to land to carry out "alteration, adjustment or improvements" necessary to preserve adjoining land.

③ Entry by Licence:
A bare licence can be revoked at will. A licence by contract may be revoked unless it was given for a specific purpose and a limited time.

NB... The trespasser must be given a reasonable time to leave.

Trespass to Goods

Another type of interference with possession is Trespass to Goods

> Trespass to goods is the unauthorised touching of someone else's property, for example...
> Snatching someone's hat
> kicking someone's dog
> erasing a tape-recording
> Scratching the panel of a vehicle

"But I thought it was mine!"

Touching someone else's goods mistakenly will still count as trespass, since you <u>intended</u> to touch the goods.

> Even if the goods are yours, you can be liable for trespass if you seize them from someone who has lawful possession of them (eg. if they are holding them as a bailee until you pay money owing to them)

"Can a dog commit the tort of trespass to goods?"

"Yes, if for example you trained it to fetch someone else's golf balls."

<u>Manton v. Brocklebank 1923</u>

QUIZ - TRESPASS

1. If you wander onto private property by mistake, you may be liable for trespass to land

   True / False ?

2. If you use the highway for a purpose such as spying on a neighbour, you may be liable for trespass to land

   True / False ?

3. On a building site, a large crane swings over the airspace of adjoining land; although it does not physically touch the property this could still be trespass.

   True / False ?

4. A guest in a hotel can bring an action against someone trespassing in his/her room

   True / False ?

5. By showing a private letter to someone not authorised to see it, you may be liable for trespass to goods.

   True / False ?

CHAPTER NINE: STRICT LIABILITY - The Rule in Rylands v Fletcher

Blackburn J: "A person who for his own purposes brings on his land anything likely to do mischief if it escapes must keep it in at his peril."

If the "dangerous" thing escapes, and damage was foreseeable, the owner will be liable for all the consequences, even if he took all due care, and wasn't negligent.

To be liable under this rule...

- The thing causing damage must be brought onto the land, and not occur there naturally.

- It must be foreseeable that the thing could cause damage eg. fireworks, chemicals, gas

Blackburn J. — The rule covers "The person whose grass or corn is eaten by the escaping cattle of his neighbour, or whose mine is flooded by the water from his neighbour's reservoir or whose cellar is invaded by the filth of his neighbour's privy"

- There must be an "escape" of the dangerous thing from the defendant's land.

"I'm suing under the rule in Rylands v. Fletcher"

"You can't, the dangerous thing didn't escape from the land"

Read v. J Lyons & Co. Ltd 1947

It must be shown that there was a "non-natural" use of the land. As Lord Moulton said in 1913

> It is not every use to which land is put that brings into play that principle. It must be some special use, bringing with it increased danger to others.

> Are there any times when the occupier isn't liable under the rule in <u>Rylands v. Fletcher</u>?

① If the plaintiff consented to the dangerous thing being kept there, and the defendant wasn't negligent in doing so.

② If the escape was due to the act of a stranger, or an act of God which couldn't have been foreseen or prevented.

③ If the defendant was under a statutory duty to do something, and he wasn't negligent in doing so.

<u>Cambridge Water v. Eastern Counties Leather 1994</u>

It was held in the above case that strict liability for the escape from land of things likely to do mischief only arose if the defendant knew or ought reasonably to have foreseen that those things might, if they escaped, cause damage.

Lord Goff →

> It by no means follows that the defendant should be liable for damage of a type which could not be reasonably foreseeable.

Liability for fire

The **Fires Prevention (Metropolis) Act 1774** states that No action shall lie against anyone in whose building or on whose estate a fire shall accidentally begin.

"Does that also mean a fire which was begun negligently?"

"No, 'accidentally' means a fire produced by mere chance or incapable of being traced to any cause"

← Lord Denman CJ

The defendant will not be liable under this act if in the absence of negligence...

a fire broke out due to defective wiring

a household fire spread when a spark fell out of the grate

The defendant will be liable however, if once the fire has begun, he takes no steps to put it out.

The occupier may be liable if his employer, guest or independent contractor negligently starts a fire which damages other property.

"I will not be liable, however, if it started due to the act of a stranger, such as a trespasser, over which I had no control."

Liability for Animals

The *Animals Act 1971* imposes strict liability on keepers of dangerous animals, and sometimes on keepers of non-dangerous animals

s. 2(1) The keeper is strictly liable for damage caused by dangerous animals (eg. tigers, snakes etc.)

s. 2(2) The keeper is strictly liable for damage caused by NON dangerous types of animals (dogs, horses etc.) if the damage was caused by a characteristic not typical in animals of that species, and that characteristic was known to the owner.

Who is the "keeper" of the animal?

s.6 - The keeper is the person who owns the animal, or keeps it in his possession. If the animal is kept by someone who is under sixteen, the owner will be the head of that household.

  Abandoning an animal does not mean the owner is no longer responsible for it. Responsibility will remain with the owner, until another person becomes the owner.

Defences under this Act

I'm not liable for damage caused wholly due to the plaintiff's fault

The keeper is not liable for damage caused to a trespasser if the dog was not a guard dog, or if it was a guard dog there would be no liability if it was not unreasonable to keep it there.

QUIZ - STRICT LIABILITY
(The rule in Rylands v. Fletcher, fire, animals)

① If poisonous vegetation grew out from your land into a neighbour's land, you may be liable under the rule in <u>Rylands v. Fletcher</u> for any resulting damage.

True / False ?

② If someone owned a tame elephant, bred in captivity, it may not be judged as a dangerous animal, due to its peaceful nature.

True / False ?

③ If earth and rocks fell from a cliff-face, injuring a person on the neighbouring land, would the landowner be liable under the rule in <u>Rylands v. Fletcher</u> ?

Yes / No

CHAPTER TEN: VICARIOUS LIABILITY

Vicarious liability means to have personal liability for the torts committed by someone else. It most often arises in the case of an employer and an employee.

"When will I be vicariously liable for another person's torts?"

If that person is an employee and they were acting in the course of employment.

For example, if a bus driver runs over a passenger, the bus company will be liable to the injured person if the driver was negligent.

"By making the employer vicariously liable, the injured person has a better chance of recovering damages in all cases, and it is an incentive to the employer to provide better care and safety at work."

The employer may then bring an action to recover damages from the employee.

In what type of circumstances may vicarious liability also arise?
- If the employee carries out the authorised task, but in a wrongful manner
- When the employee acts negligently or disobediently
- When the employee makes a mistake.

47

When is the employee acting "in the course of employment"?

If a bus driver negligently injures someone while driving a bus, his employers will be vicariously liable. Not all situations are so straightforward, however...

Expressly Prohibited Conduct

RULE No. 865 — DRIVERS MUST NOT RACE WITH OTHER BUSES

If a bus driver disobeyed this rule, and injured someone while racing with another bus, would the employer be vicariously liable?

In the above case, the employers were vicariously liable, because the driver was allowed to drive buses. He was doing what he was authorised to do, but in an improper way. Such disobedience did not take him outside the course of employment.

Limpus v. London General Omnibus Co. 1862

Mistake

"But you're on the wrong train!"

A passenger was roughly pulled off a train by a porter, who mistakenly believed he was on the wrong train.

It was held that the company were vicariously liable for their employee's mistakes, since he was acting in the course of employment at the time.

Bayley v. Manchester, Sheffield and Lincolnshire Ry 1873

If it can be shown that he was doing something wrong, but it was done in the interests of his employers, the employers may be vicariously liable.

When is the employee NOT acting within the course of employment?

When he does something he is not authorised to do?

A bus conductor tried to turn the bus around, and caused an accident. His employers were not liable since he was authorised only to collect fares, not drive buses. *Beard v. London General Omnibus Co. 1900*

When he is not acting in the interests of his employer

Contrast

Case 1: An employee struck a boy who fell and was injured, because he believed he was stealing sugar from the stall. The employers were liable. *Poland v. John Parr & Sons 1927*

Case 2: A petrol pump attendant began to argue with a customer about payment. The argument became personal, and the employee struck the customer. The employers were not vicariously liable. *Warren v. Henlys Ltd 1948*

What was the difference?
In the first case the employee was protecting his employer's property when he struck the boy. In the second case, the fight had become of a personal nature.

When he is taking a Detour

If someone is employed to drive from A to B, the employer will probably be liable for any accidents he causes along the way. If, however, he decides to take a detour to C, solely for his own personal benefit, the employer will not be liable for any torts the employee commits whilst "on a frolic of his own".

Who is an employee?

To decide this, it is necessary to distinguish between:
- A contract of service (for employees)
- A contract for services (for independent contractors)

An employer will not usually be liable for torts of independent contractors.

To decide whether there is a contract of service, the courts look at a number of factors:
- Is the employee's work an integral part of the business?
- Does the employer pay wages, and National Insurance contributions?
- Can the employer dismiss the worker?
- The control test

What is the control test?

"We look to see whether the employer controls the type of work done, and how it is done (unless it involves highly skilled work.)"

Yewen v. Noakes 1880

In *Market Investigations Ltd v. Minister of Social Security 1969* it was decided:

The test for whether a contract of service exists is to see whether the worker is doing the task as part of his own business on his own account, for reward.

"But this test is not conclusive"

QUIZ - VICARIOUS LIABILITY

① A lorry driver took a detour to his house to collect his spectacles whilst making a delivery. He could not drive safely without them, he said. On the way back from his house he had an accident. Were his employers vicariously liable? Yes / No

② A cleaning lady was sent to offices late at night to clear up. While there, instead of cleaning, she made telephone calls totalling £1,500. Were the agency who employed her vicariously liable? Yes / No

③ A driver of a petrol tanker was waiting in the petrol station, while the tanks were being filled from his tanker. He lit a cigarette and threw the match on the floor causing an explosion. His employers were vicariously liable since he was doing his job at the time. True / False?

④ A customer had an argument with a barmaid, and allegedly insulted her. She reacted by throwing a glass of beer in his face. Were her employers vicariously liable for her act? Yes / No

CHAPTER ELEVEN: THE EMPLOYER'S DUTY

The employer also owes a duty to the employee under the common law

The duty the employer owes at common law is basically to make sure the employee is not exposed to unnecessary risks.

The duty was defined as

"The provision of a competent staff of men, adequate material and a proper system and effective supervision."

Wilsons and Clyde Coal Co. Ltd v. English 1938

So if, for example, someone is injured due to the incompetence or negligence of a fellow workman, the employer is liable under the common law duty of care.

"I will have discharged my common law duty if I exercise reasonable care in all these areas."

"What's the difference between an employer's common law duty, and vicarious liability, for a careless workman who injures someone?"

To be vicariously liable for his employee's torts, the employee must have been acting in the course of employment. The common law duty is much wider, and will cover situations when this can't be shown.

Safe Equipment

"I must make sure I provide protective clothing and equipment for my employees and if necessary, ensure they are being used."

The Employers' Liability (Defective Equipment) Act 1969
This act states that if anyone is injured at work by defective equipment, the employer may be strictly liable.

Safe Premises and a Proper System of Work

"It is my duty to make sure everything is running smoothly and safely, and all instructions regarding safety are being obeyed."

Delegating the duty

"But I told him to check everything was safe"

"The duty on the employer is personal, and cannot be delegated to anyone else."

QUIZ - THE EMPLOYER'S DUTY

1. An employee would clean windows by balancing on a window sill. The employers knew about this, but did nothing to stop it. One day, the employee slipped and fell. Were the employers liable?

    Yes / No

2. An employee often played practical jokes on his fellow employees. He was warned about this, but did not stop, and one day his horseplay resulted in fracturing a fellow employee's wrist. Were the employers liable?

    Yes / No

3. If the employer appoints someone else to check that everything is safe, the employer will no longer be liable for any accidents that occur.

    True / False

4. Once the employer has provided a safe system of work, they are under no duty to check their employees are using it properly.

    True / False

CHAPTER TWELVE : DEFAMATION

When is a statement defamatory?

The court must consider whether publication of the statement would damage a person's reputation, causing people to shun or avoid him. In the words of Lord Atkin...

Would the words tend to lower the plaintiff in the estimation of right-thinking members of society generally?

The statement must be communicated to a third party in order for it to be actionable, and this is so both for libel and slander.

libel →

If the defamatory statement is in permanent form, it will be libel, and is actionable per se (ie. without proof of special damage)

Anything defamatory which is in the form of spoken words or gestures will be slander...

← Slander

Who decides if the words are defamatory?

The judge decides if the words are capable or not of having a defamatory meaning.

If so, it's up to the jury to decide if they are defamatory in this case.

"But no one believed it!"

"It doesn't matter. If the words were defamatory and published to a third party, it makes no difference if they believed them or not."

Are there any defences to Defamation?

① "Sorry, I didn't mean it..." — If the statement was published innocently, and the defendant does his/her best to amend the situation, according to the Defamation Act 1952. s.4, this may be a defence.

② FAIR COMMENT — If the statement was a comment based on true facts, and made as a matter of public interest, this will be a defence, unless it was actuated by malice.

③ JUSTIFICATION — If the defendant can prove the statement was true, justification can be a defence.

④ ABSOLUTE PRIVILEGE — If the comment was made in the course of parliamentary proceedings or judicial proceedings, (when relevant to the trial), or if it was made between solicitor and client, this may be a defence.

⑤ QUALIFIED PRIVILEGE — Covers many numerous situation.

QUIZ - DEFAMATION

1. If you found a waxwork of yourself in Madame Tussauds, this could be a case of libel

   True / False ?

2. Calling someone rude names will be defamation.

   True / False ?

3. If something defamatory is written about you, in a foreign language, this will still be libel if no one who reads it understands it.

   True / False ?

4. If you repeat something defamatory you heard about another person, you will not be liable for defamation, since you are merely repeating another person's words.

   True / False ?

5. If a newspaper publishes a statement about someone which is true, justification will be no defence to an action for defamation, if it was actuated by malice.

   True / False ?

6. An action for defamation will be tried by jury

   True / False ?

QUIZ ANSWERS

Chapter One - Trespass to the Person

① False. It's only an assault if you believed it to be loaded.
② False. These were the facts of a case Wilkinson v. Downton 1897. Words can be actionable in tort if they were intended to cause harm, and they did result in physical harm to the plaintiff.
③ True - although you would probably receive only nominal damages.
④ False. You are entitled to strike the first blow in self-defence.
⑤ True. These were the facts of Warner v. Riddiford 1858, where the plaintiff successfully sued her ex-employer for false imprisonment.

Chapter Two - Negligence - The Duty of Care

① Yes, since she'd come upon them when they were still in the same state they'd been in at the scene of the accident (McLoughlin v O'Brien)
② False. Although he was a close relation, he would still have to prove there was a bond of love and affection between them.
③ True. This happened in a case Attia v. British Gas 1988.
④ False. It was decided in Rondel v. Worsley 1969 that a barrister is immune when acting in court, but could be liable for negligence for work done out of court.
⑤ False. There is no liability for failing to act, unless you had caused the situation to arise, by pushing them in, for example, or a special relationship existed, such as parent and child.

QUIZ ANSWERS

Chapter Three - Negligence - Breach of duty

① True — He could be liable, as he would be judged by the standard of an ordinary, reasonable driver - Roberts v. Ramsbottom 1980

② No — The risk would be weighed against the cost and practicability of eradicating it. Closing the factory down was the only way to eliminate the risk completely, which was too drastic in this case. (Latimer v. AEC Ltd 1953)

③ No — Whether a doctor is a junior, or has twenty years' experience, the standard they're judged by is of an ordinary doctor. (Wilsher v. Essex Area Health Authority 1987)

④ No — The precautions taken were adequate when measured against the risk (Bolton v. Stone)

Chapter Four - Negligence - That Results in Damage

① Yes — Injury by burning was foreseeable, therefore it made no difference if it happened in an unexpected way.

② False — B's act was foreseeable, and to be expected, and would not break the chain of causation.

③ False — It will not necessarily be so, there is always the risk that someone may receive negligent medical treatment, which A may be liable for.

④ Yes — But not, however, if the event was entirely unexpected, such as if squatters moved in (Stansbie v. Troman 1948)

QUIZ ANSWERS

Chapter Five - The Defences

① **False** — A child could be guilty of contributory negligence if the danger was very obvious (McKinnell v. White 1971)

② **False** — Any sign like this, on business premises, would be completely void by s. 2(1), of the Unfair Contract Terms Act 1977. The shop owners would be liable for injury caused through negligence.

③ **False** — A child may be guilty of contributory negligence. Lord Denning said, however, that this should only be if he or she is "blameworthy", and the standard they are judged against is an ordinary child of that age.

④ **False** — You may be held to be contributorily negligent, but knowledge of the risk you are taking, does not necessarily imply consent to it.

Chapter Six - Occupier's Liability

① **True** — If a person begins a fire negligently, he or she may be liable if the fireman is injured putting it out (Ogwo v. Taylor 1988)

② **No** — Under the 1984 act, a trespasser can only recover damages for injury to the person. Under the 1957 act, damage to property is also recoverable.

③ **False** — The occupier can expect a specialist to be aware of the dangers of their trade (Roles v. Nathan 1963)

④ **False** — This is because the visitor had no choice but to use that bridge. Had the sign indicated another bridge to use, the occupier would escape liability.

QUIZ ANSWERS

Chapter Seven - Nuisance

① False — Unpleasant smells can be actionable as nuisance.

② False — 'Coming to the nuisance' is no defence, and you can never gain a right by prescription to do something which is a public nuisance.

③ No — You cannot increase your neighbour's liability by putting your own premises to extra-special use.
(Robinson v. Kilvert 1889)

④ False — As Wray CJ said in 1587, "the law does not give an action for such things of delight"

Chapter Eight - Trespass

① True — Even if you made a genuine mistake, your action was still voluntary, and intentional.

② True — In Hickman v. Maisey the defendant walked up and down the highway, in order to spy on a rival's racehorses. He was held liable for trespass to the subsoil.

③ True — It is trespass to airspace, and the plaintiff may be granted an injunction (Wooleiton v. Constain 1970)

④ False

⑤ True (Thurston v. Charles 1905)

QUIZ ANSWERS

Chapter Nine – Strict Liability – The rule in Rylands v Fletcher – Liability for fire and animals

① True — This was decided in <u>Crowhurst v. Amersham Burial Board 1878</u> and <u>Ponting v. Noakes 1895</u>.

② False — In <u>Behrens v. Bertram Mills Circus Ltd 1957</u>, the owner of a circus elephant was liable for injuries it caused, even though it was said to be "no more dangerous than a cow".

③ No — There has to be an escape of objects not naturally on the land. The owner may, however, be liable in nuisance.

Chapter Ten – Vicarious Liability

① Yes — He was getting his spectacles in order to drive more safely, and had not taken the detour solely for his own benefit (Angus v. Glasgow Corporation 1977)

② No — Making phone calls was not an act done in the course of her employment – she was authorised to clean the phone, but not to use it

③ True — His act of lighting a cigarette was done while he was carrying out his work, and could not be separated from it. (Century Insurance Co. Ltd v. Northern Ireland Road Transport Board 1942)

④ No — Her act was one connected with a personal argument, and thus not done in the course of employment.

QUIZ ANSWERS

Chapter Eleven - The Employer's Duty

① Yes. They were under a duty to provide a safe system of work.

② Yes. They were under a duty to provide competent staff. They knew about the horseplay.

③ False. The duty is personal, and cannot be delegated.

④ False. The employer is under a duty not just to provide a safe system of work, but also to check it is being carried out.

Chapter Twelve - Defamation

① True. This happened in the case <u>Monson v Tussauds 1894</u>, it was decided that waxworks, statues, or even chalk marks could be libel.

② False. Insults would not usually be defamatory, unless they affected a person's reputation.

③ False. Just as it wouldn't be libel if no one ever read it.

④ False. You will be liable for defamation in the same way as the original maker of the statement.

⑤ False. Justification is a complete defence, unlike fair comment, which is defeated if malice is proved.

⑥ True. It's one of the rare civil cases which is tried by jury.

INDEX

Animals, liability for, 45
Assault, 1
Battery, 2
Breach of duty, 12-16
Care - see duty of care
Children, and negligence, 15
    Occupiers' liability for, 30
Contributory Negligence, 24, 31
Defamation, 55
    defences to, 56
Defences, animals, liability for, 45
    consent, 4, 29, 35
    contributory negligence, 24, 31
    defamation, 56
    ex turpi causa, 27
    lawful arrest, 4
    nuisance, 36
    Occupiers' Liability Act 1957, 31
    Occupiers' Liability Act 1984, 32
Duty of Care, 6-11
    breach of, 12-16
    damage caused by breach, 17-23
    res ipsa loquitur, 20
    economic loss, 8
    negligent misstatement, 9
    neighbour principle, 6
    nervous shock, 10

    reasonable man, 12
    risk, 13, 14
Economic Loss, 8
'Egg Shell Skull' rule, 22
Employers' Liability, at common law, 52-54
    vicarious liability, 47-51
Ex Turpi Causi, 27
False Imprisonment, 3
    defences to, 4
Fire, escape of, 44
Illegality, 27
Independent contractors, liability for, 50
Intervening Causes, 22-24
Justification, 56
Liability for animals, 45
Libel, 55
Negligence, 6-23
    breach of duty, 12-16
    causation, 17-22
    economic loss, 8
    'egg shell skull' rule, 22
    negligent misstatement, 9
    neighbour principle, 6
    nervous shock, 10
    novus actus interveniens, 19
    reasonable man, 12
    risk, 13, 14

social utility, 14
Nervous shock, 10
Novus Actus Interveniens, 19
Nuisance, 34-37
    private, 35
    defences to, 36
    public, 34
Occupiers' Liability, 29-33
    Occupiers' Liability Act 1957, 29
    duty owed to children, 30
    duty owed to skilled visitors, 30
    defences, 31
    Occupiers' Liability Act 1984, 32
    defences to, 31
Private nuisance, 35
Professionals and negligence, 15
Psychiatric damage, 10
Public nuisance, 34
Reasonable man, 12
Remoteness of damage, 21
Res Ipsa Loquitur, 20
Rescuers, 26
Risk, negligence, 13, 14
Rylands v. Fletcher, 42-43
Slander, 55
Standard of care, 6-11
Strict liability, 42-46
    animals, 45

fire, escape of, 44
Rylands v. Fletcher, 42-43
Trespass to goods, 40
Trespass to land, 38
    defences to, 39
Trespass to the person, 1-5
    assault, 1
    battery, 2
    defences to, 4
    false imprisonment, 3
Vicarious liability, 47-51
    acting in the course of employment, 48-9
    independent contractors, 50
Volenti non fit injuria, 25-31
    and rescuers, 26